7 MYTHS

ABOUT

AQUAPONICS

Michelle Booth

COO FARM PRESS

7 MYTHS ABOUT AQUAPONICS
An introduction to aquaponics for beginners
3nd Edition May 2013

Michelle Booth

A Coo Farm Press Beginners Guide

LEGAL NOTICE & DISCLAIMER

The author and publisher have used their best efforts in preparing this book and the information provided herein is provided "as is", making no representation or warranties with respect to the accuracy or completeness of the contents of this book and specifically disclaim any implied warranties or merchantability or fitness for any particular purpose and shall in no event be liable for any loss of profit or any other personal or commercial damage, including but not limited to special, incidental, consequential or other damages.

Much of this publication is based on personal experience and anecdotal evidence. Although the author and publisher have made every reasonable attempt to achieve complete accuracy of the content in this book, they assume no responsibility for errors or omissions. You should use this information as you see fit and at your own risk. Your particular situation may not be exactly suited to the examples illustrated here and you should adjust your use of the information and recommendations accordingly.

ISBN-13: 978-1484974117
ISBN-10: 1484974115

DEDICATION

This book is dedicated to my friend and
coach Jane Vigon, who gave me back my
confidence and restored my interest in
pursuing a healthy lifestyle.

CONTENTS

INTRODUCTION

Aquaponics ... it sounds like something from Star Trek. In Star Trek Voyager, Kes sets up a very prolific hydroponic garden on the starship when the replicators stop working and food supplies dwindle. Actually, the stuff on Star Trek is hydroponics – growing plants without soil, in nutrient-rich fluid. It isn't fiction, NASA use both hydroponics and aquaponics, calling them 'Farming For The Future'.

Although it sounds very 21-century, it isn't a new technology. The first experiments with growing plants without soil actually took place back in the 1600s. That isn't a misprint - the **sixteen** hundreds!

The problem with hydroponics is that it needs a lot of human intervention, and a lot of chemicals. Bottles and bottles of chemicals.

Aquaponics is different – it uses a combination of hydroponics and aquaculture (fish farming). The fish and plants work symbiotically – each feed the other. It's a self-contained ecosystem that requires little human intervention (we don't need to fiddle with it!). So we don't need to add nutrients to the plants, the fish do that. We don't need to add chemicals to control the water quality, the plants do that. The plants act like a reed bed, filtering and purifying the water.

The result is happy fish, happy plants and very happy humans. A happy planet, too, as there is no waste (the plants need the waste products from the fish, they make them grow) and very little environmental impact. Aquaculture does have environmental impact, because the fish waste is a problem.

Growing plants aquaponically uses 90% less water than growing them in soil, so it is ideal for areas of drought and water supply problems.

It is organic – it has to be, you can't use pesticides on the plants in an aquaponics system as it would kill the fish.

It is possible for people to garden aquaponically who can't garden traditionally, due to the lack of need for digging, weeding, bending, and risks associated with using pesticides.

When people first get interested in aquaponics they often start with an Internet search and can get disheartened. It is easy to be baffled by all the information out there, there is such a lot of it, much of it confusing, contradictory and overly technical. The dream of setting up your own system can seem very far off.

People can be scared by the electrical components of aquaponics – after all, water and electricity aren't supposed to mix. You need a pump to get the water from the fish tank to the growbed. When I first looked into getting an aquaponic system, this did frighten me. Then I got engaged to a wonderful man - who happened to be a qualified electrician! When I found out I thought, "Great! I can finally get into aquaponics!"

I soon found out, though, that the electrical parts are actually really simple and all enclosed and water-tight. They are designed to live in water and the parts that plug into the mains electricity don't go near the water.

It only took me a short while - after seeing him set up a system - to gain the confidence to try setting one up myself.

Once you get your own system you realize it's a little like using a computer. You don't have to fully understand a computer to use it; neither do you have to fully understand about pumps, siphons and drains to use an aquaponics system.

I love the fact that my family has a source of healthy, organic plants growing whenever we need them, all year round. It is also great to know that we are doing our bit to reduce food miles and saving some money at the same time.

I wrote this little book to dispel some of the myths surrounding aquaponics, because I'd love to see more people take up the hobby. It is a way to get fresh, healthy produce if you are concerned about fears of genetic modification and manipulation by food producers.

I've covered the big seven myths, as well as the most frequently-asked questions by beginners and those just starting out on their aquaponics journey.

Let's look at an aquaponics system as being like the hardware and software of a computer system:

- On a computer the hardware is the monitor, tower, keyboard, mouse, etc. The software is the stuff that makes it work, that makes each component communicate and lets you get information in and out of the system.

- In an aquaponics system the hardware parts are the fish tank, the growbed, the electrical bits (pump, hoses and drain) and the growbed medium (e.g. clay pebbles). The software, the stuff that makes the whole thing work, are the fish and the plants.

The best part is this ... everything is plug & play! I'm OK with computers, I don't fully understand how they work, but I can make them do the things I need to. It is exactly the same with my aquaponic system.

If you are going to use a ready-made system, all you have to do is put the tanks in place (systems often come with a stand so the growbed sits above the fish tank), put the pump in the fish tank and thread the hose up into the growbed, then slot the drain on. Hands-on courses are great for giving you the confidence to try this yourself. If you don't have access to one, there is a very good, comprehensive course on Udemy (http://ude.my/c47ef).

You could create your own DIY system if you are good at making things. Many systems use a principle of flood & drain, which is easy to understand. The water is pumped up onto the growbed and when it reaches a certain level the drain (which sits in a hole in the bottom of the growbed) is triggered, which releases the water back down into the fish tank.

An investment of small amount of money will reward you many, many times over with herbs, vegetables, fruits and fish. If you want to, you can choose edible fish. If you don't, you can have them as pets.

What you don't have is a horrid chore each week of cleaning out that tank, as you would with an aquarium. With aquaponics, it's hands-off as much as possible. Cleaning the tank would mess up the ecosystem. You want the beneficial bacteria that grow in there because they break down the fish waste into usable nutrients for the plants.

I don't claim to be an aquaponics expert (you don't need to be to have a healthy aquaponics system), and I haven't written this book as a complete 'How To'. What I wanted to do was dispel some of the myths and explain how easy it is to get up and running with a system.

This is just a, 'If I can do it you can too' book!

So let's look at some myths surrounding aquaponics.

PART ONE

THE MYTHS

MYTH 1 - YOU NEED TO BE A FISH EXPERT

If you have ever tried to keep tropical fish – or even the odd goldfish – you may be put off trying aquaponics due to the problems you've experienced.

Swim bladder, fish swimming in circles, on their sides, swellings and growths, dead fish, the list goes on. Perhaps you had a kitchen window ledge like a drugstore, with medicines for various fishy ailments such as swim bladder and white spot and different potions for altering the pH of the water, the nitrate content of the water, the wateriness of the water. It can seem that you can never get the water just right for the little blighters.

Maybe you got fed up of waiting for the kids to keep their fervent promise to clean the aquarium every week and you ended up doing it yourself and cleaning a month's worth of gunge out of the filters and off the glass every time.

Who could blame you for thinking that aquaponics is going to be like that with a few lettuce thrown in?

The good news – no, the great news – is that Aquaponics is different! It is as far removed from keeping an aquarium as keeping lions on a safari is from keeping a domesticated moggy in a small home. The domesticated cat will scratch your furniture (and possibly your legs), require regular de-fleaing and de-worming, need meals served twice a day in a special bowl from expensive little tins with gold edges, and use a box filled with bought litter that you have to clean out frequently before it stinks the house out, etc.

The lions? You just drive through their paddock in a LandRover once a day and bung half an unfortunate cow out the back for them to scrap over. The lions in the safari paddock look after themselves, pretty much. The domesticated cat wants to be waited on hand and paw.

The aquaponics system is like a self-managing microclimate. It is a complete system on its own - a safari on its own if we continue the analogy.

You feed the fish, the fish feed the plants, the plants nourish the fish and finally the plants feed you. It's a complete system.

If you have had an aquarium you will know that adding plants to the water helps water quality and fish health. Imagine adding a whole rack of plants. That's what you do with an aquaponics system.

Look at the image below. The fish live in the bottom tank and the plants live in the top one. It's actually quite simple.

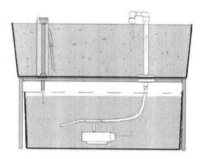

The fish produce waste, which is converted by bacteria in the water into nitrites and nitrates - food for the plants.

The nutrient-rich water is pumped from the bottom tank into the top tank. It oozes through the plants and their roots, supplying them with nutrients (they actually LIKE fish waste!) and water. The water then drains through the plants roots and the growing medium down into the fish tank again. The plant roots act like a reed bed, filtering and purifying the water. The cleaned water keeps the fish happy and healthy.

All you need to do is keep a check on the water using simple, inexpensive kits, feed the fish and harvest the plants.

You will need to clean the tank occasionally (but you don't need to disinfect it), especially if you have an outside system as bits of leaves and debris always manage to work their way in somehow. But it's a whole lot easier to clean a big tank than a fiddly little aquarium – especially those odd-shaped ones that children are drawn to! It's more like a garden pond, all you need to do is brush the sides and bottom of the tank. The water goes a bit cloudy but soon clears.

Aquaponics systems get better with age. You don't want too much human intervention. It's better to let the system do the work and only intervene when necessary.

If you were to replace the water, for example, you would be getting rid of the vital bacteria that are needed to convert the fish waste into nutrients for the plants.

So you don't have to be a fish expert. Let nature be the expert.

There are some things you need to do to help fish health and your fish supplier is a good place to start.

There are also aquaponics courses available in many countries which give more information but here are a few tips:

- Prepare the tank. Fill it with water* and start the pump. Let it run and start the cycling process before adding fish. Check it is ready by testing the water.
- Don't over-stock your fish. Each fish needs approximately two and a half gallons of water space.
- Only buy fish from reputable breeders. Garden centers can be good sources but they aren't always.
- Check the condition of the fish and their tanks before buying. Look out for unhealthy-looking fish, dead fish, debris in the tanks, stuff growing on the walls of the tanks.

- Make sure you follow the standard instructions when bringing your fish home. Place the unopened bag in the aquaponics tank for 15-30 minutes before letting the fish out. Think about it – if you had travelled home in a hot car for an hour or so and then plunged into a cold pool in the garden it would be a bit of a shock. It's the same for the scaly guys. Allowing them to acclimatize to their new environment is a very important first step.

- Buy some food from the fish breeder. It's what the fish will be used to and this will help them settle in. If you want to switch later on you can do it gradually so they won't become temperamental gourmets.

- Don't overfeed. Overfeeding is one of the biggest causes of ill-health in fish (and probably in humans too but let's not go there!). Follow the instructions on the fish food and watch them occasionally. If they are leaving food, you are giving them too much. Overfeeding can alter the pH level of the water.

- Check the water weekly using a simple, easy-to-use, inexpensive test kit.
- Check that the water is being aerated. If it has bubbles it is. They could come from an air stone, or the fall of the water from the growbed.
- Don't panic. Relax safe in the knowledge that the plants will be making the water healthy for the fish and the fish have a great environment.

*There has been a query over use of water from some deep wells in aquaponics systems, due to the high salt content in the water. To be safe, have your water checked by your fish supplier.

MYTH 2 – YOU CAN'T DO AQUAPONICS IF YOU ARE VEGETARIAN OR VEGAN

Vegetarians and particularly vegans have concerns when thinking about setting up their own aquaponics system, apart from, obviously, not wanting to eat fish themselves:

- About whether the fish are harmed;
- If the plants can be considered edible for a vegan, with the nutrients that sustained them having "gone through" fishes' digestive systems;
- If the fish food is vegetarian.

The answers to these issues won't be the same for everyone. We are all at different stages in our journeys.

ARE THE FISH HARMED?

Some people choose to eat the fish in their aquaponics system – but you don't have to.

You can give your fish a potentially long, happy, and healthy life in your aquaponics system, secure in the knowledge that their needs are being met and that you aren't being cruel to them. In fact, you would be giving them a much better life than they would have had if they had been bought by someone to put in their little aquarium.

Are Fish-Fed Plants OK For Vegetarians/Vegans?

A lot of this is down to personal choice and bcliefs.

For example, as a vegetarian with vegan leanings myself, I don't buy eggs from the supermarket. I have my own chickens and only eat their eggs. They are fed purchased chicken food topped up with green plants from my aquaponics system.

I do have an aquaponics system but I don't eat my own fish.

I try as much as I can to avoid any commercial food production systems and growing my own produce is kinder to the environment than buying foods that have come from the other side of the planet.

Aquaponics supplies you with a clean, unprocessed, organic food source that doesn't harm anyone or anything – animals, fish, third-world farmers, the environment. That's something most vegetarians and vegans are very keen on. Where we draw the line between using animals and including them in our lifestyle choices though, is where we differ. But generally, we can agree to differ!

As vegetarians, we often talk about how much better vegetarianism is for the planet. Much more food can be grown on an acre of land than can be produced from cows occupying that acre. Imagine how much produce could be grown if that acre was full of aquaponics systems – around 10 times as much.

Or, even better, if everyone had their own aquaponics system in their back yard and took control of their health and nutrition back from big pharmaceutical companies.

There is talk of using aquaponics systems in Japan where the land was contaminated by radiation after the 2011 earthquake and tsunami and resultant fallout from the Fukushima power plant.

That's where you start to realize the enormous potential of aquaponics – as a way of growing clean, pure produce even in contaminated areas.

The 2011 earthquake in Japan caused radiation contamination after the fallout from the Fukushima power plant, and a tsunami which contaminated the land.

The Japanese website Japan-Aquaponics reports that: 'In Fukushima, certain areas will be unable to grow crops for decades to come due to the radiation in the soil, and in all of the areas that were inundated by the tsunami ... the salt levels in the soil will make growing certain crops very difficult and at the very least will result in significantly reduced crop yields.'

Japan-Aquaponics are fundraising for donations to help the stricken people in those areas, by supplying the farmers with aquaponics systems. They can, of course, grow food safely aquaponically because it doesn't need the contaminated soil to produce the crops.

That is the future of aquaponics. Making a difference. Something vegetarians and vegans identify with.

IS FISH FOOD VEGETARIAN?

Not usually – unless you look for it. Fish need protein and commercial fish food is largely made up of other fish – because that is the natural diet of some fish.

At the moment, I do feed my fish commercial fish food as they aren't vegetarian fish and fish meal is very low down on the list of ingredients of their food (rice is first). That's something that my vegan friends would definitely avoid though. I am on the look-out for a fish food that I feel happier with, and not just because of my personal vegan leanings.

MYTH 3 – IT'S HARD WORK

This is the really good one! Aquaponics is so easy that it's almost child's play.

Perhaps this myth arose from people trying to start by building their own systems, without plans and support. That would be a bit tricky for those who aren't competent at building things themselves and don't have access to plans and advice.

Or perhaps it was from people who have set up large commercial-sized operations. That would be a lot of work!

Setting up an aquaponics system really isn't difficult – especially if you buy a system - and the initial set-up can be done in less than an hour.

It isn't difficult to run a system either – you don't have to water the plants manually (other than setting up the water pump), all you need to do is feed the fish. Even the feeding of the fish can be automated if you want to get a bit more technical. Personally, I rather like feeding the fish. They are quite comical and it is a good time to have a look at them to make sure they are healthy.

All you need to do is ensure that the fish needs are being met. Their needs are very simple - food (feed them) and oxygen (keep the pump running). The only other tasks are checking the water (weekly, using an easy-to-use kit – it takes just a couple of minutes) and harvesting the plants (the fun part!).

For holidays, the system can be left with slow-release fish food blocks in the water. You don't have to worry about the fish or the plants. In fact, fish will live without food for several weeks so you don't even need to add the blocks. We tend to, so we don't have to worry about getting held up when we are away (we caravan, so we sometimes stay an extra night or two if we find a great site and the weather is good).

I still do some traditional gardening, in my raised bed and in pots and potato bags. Boy does it seem like hard work compared to my aquaponics gardening! I pulled some big weeds out of my raised bed last week (after hunting for ages for my gardening gloves, which one of the dogs had run off with!) and this week the dratted weeds are back again, with friends.

It's hard to get the water right for the potatoes in bags. They need a lot of water but too much can rot them and if you go out for the day and it turns unexpectedly hot, the poor plants are all wilted and dropping over the sides of the bags when you get back.

Not so the aquaponics crops. They get soaked and drained every 15 minutes with nutrient-rich water (fish-waste water!), which makes them bloom and thrive. You can almost watch them grow! The water only floods their roots, so I've never had any problem with the leaves getting scorched, which can happen if garden plants get their leaves wet on hot days.

We have had a scare, when the initial batch of fish died and when we couldn't find out why for a while. It is worth it though, as you pick up so much as you start doing aquaponics and talking to others about it.

Aquaponics is hard work? That's not a myth, I think it is a lie put about by people who make money out of gardening in soil!

MYTH 4 – IT'S EXPENSIVE

All the bits for a DIY system can be bought for under $300 – absolutely everything. Buy the bits used, from thrift stores, yard sales, EBay, etc., and you could probably bring it in under $100, especially if you're good at striking a bargain.

A family-sized ready-made system will cost around $700. These are small enough to fit in a greenhouse but large enough to supply a family with all their salad produce, as well as herbs, vegetables & fruits, fresh from the system.

I'm normally asked to bring salad when I go to friends' homes for barbecues and parties, because they know how good the produce from my aquaponics system is.

Last time I forgot to harvest some, so stopped at a supermarket on the way. I picked up a bag of mixed salad greens and a bag of watercress. It came to $6. I was a bit shocked, as I haven't had to buy salads for a while!

I worked out that my family go through about 4 bags of salad a week. So if I didn't have my aquaponics system I would be spending £12 a week. That's saving me $624 per year!

And that's just the bagged salad. I also grow cucumbers – a lot of cucumbers actually, they are one of our favorite foods – broccoli, other leafy greens and fruits (strawberries do well). I try to grow things that are more expensive in the shops, so I'm saving more!

So I think the $600-odd per year saving is could actually be considerably more. But let's look at that $600. My kit cost around $700 so it almost paid for itself in its first year. The tanks and stand are very sturdy and I can see them lasting 10 years. The pump is guaranteed for 5 years. It would cost around $100 to replace, which isn't bad.

A $700 system over a minimum of 5 years, which is saving me at least $600 per year is a pretty good investment. An even better investment if I ramp up production and start selling some of my produce!

I read a book once extolling the virtues of juicers. The author said that if you could afford it, you should buy a juicer as it is one of the best tools in the kitchen to improve health. She went on to say that if you couldn't afford a juicer, to give up something else so you could still buy one – it was that important!

I'd say the same about an aquaponic system. If we looked at it purely on costs alone, it is a good investment and that's without considering the benefits of avoiding salads and other produce that have been treated with pesticides, washed in bleach (yes, really!), and scares about genetically-modified plants.

HOW TO AFFORD A SYSTEM

BUILD A DIY SYSTEM

Using second-hand parts, it is possible to build a system for around $100. Visit flea markets, yard sales, EBay, Preloved, Freecycle, and other local and online places.

Get creative – your DIY system doesn't have to look like a ready-made system.

You could use:

- A garden pond that someone is giving away on Freecycle for your fish;
- An old baby bath as your growing tank – if you have a stand for it, even better, as you can have a raised system;
- A water fountain-type pump that you pick up at a car boot sale or end-of-season sale in a garden centre;
- Some pipes and hose from a yard sale;
- A filter & drain from EBay or Craigslist.

HOW TO EARN MORE

With the economy having been messed up by the banks and the government, many people are keen to take back some power. Instead of trusting the banks to do the right thing – from risky investing in the stock market to supporting weapons sale to war-torn countries – they are taking control of their own finances.

That's commendable, but do be sure to check out reviews before committing to anything.

HOW TO AVOID SCAMS

There are ways to make extra money online but you do need to be careful to avoid scams and only use respected sites.

- If it seems too good to be true, it probably is.
- Don't part with money. Get [free] independent financial advice before investing in anything – that includes franchises, which can publish misleading information about the sort of money you can expect to make.
- Check out reviews of anything you are thinking of joining (or buying) – there will be good and bad ones. Check out several of each and make your own judgment. Remember that scam sites can post false reviews of themselves.
- Word Of Mouth – if friends (real or virtual social media friends) recommend a site, contact them personally to find out more. A post on their Facebook wall could be put there by the site itself – Inbox them and ask questions about it. Often, they won't know anything about it. They may,

however, have come across something good, and it is worth finding out more.

- Use a sacrificial email account. Money-making sites have to earn somehow and they often do so by selling their email lists – so you end up with a lot of junk email. That's fine, you can just delete the emails but use an email account that you keep specifically for this purpose, so you don't get a deluge of rubbish mixed up with your important emails.

- Don't be tempted by gambling. A dollar now and then on the lottery can quickly become $1 every time and the chances of winning are so small that it really is like throwing money away.

As interest rates are so low, people think it isn't worth putting money into savings – but even with low interest rates, saving is still better than wasting money.

If you can save $15 a week you would have enough to buy a good, family-sized aquaponics after just a year.

It's a good idea to learn about how to invest. Check out the free eBook on www.einvestingforbeginners.com.

It explains how to start investing in the stock market with minimum risk. The author doesn't trust the experts – he rightly says that financial 'experts' would give up work and be sipping cocktails on a tropical beach if their financial advice was as good as they make out! He advises people to take their finances into their own hands, learn how to analyze company data, and make investments in stocks.

If you want an aquaponics system badly enough, give your brain the task and it will come up with creative ways for you to save and make the money you need to buy the system.

When you do, start small and you could move up to a bigger system by saving the money that the system saves on your food bills!

REVIEWS/SURVEYS

The following sites are reputable and pay quite well:

- Ciao (http://bit.ly/ciao7);
- YouGov (http://bit.ly/yougov7);
- American Consumer Panel (http://bit.ly/amconsumer).

You won't make a fortune but it is a nice extra little income when times are hard.

WRITING

If you can write, you could make a good living, with the right training.

There is an excellent course teaching how to get your book written and onto Amazon Kindle. I make my living by writing, so I know it can be profitable. The course teaches you how.

Check it out at: http://ude.my/c47ew. It isn't cheap - nearly $200 – but it can teach you how to earn many, many more times that and it comes with a risk-free, 30-day money-back guarantee.

MYTH 5 – AN AQUAPONICS SYSTEM TAKES UP A LOT OF ROOM

You can have a system as large or as small as you need. There are commercial systems in huge polytunnels and there are table-top systems little bigger than a plant pot. As aquaponics becomes more popular, more of a variety of sizes of systems will become available.

My main system is about the size of two large dogs. It sits outside my back door, bubbling away cheerily. I have friends without gardens, though, who have units on balconies and in spare rooms. Some have AeroGrow units on their dining tables.

An AeroGrow Kitchen Garden system (not strictly aquaponics, this is a hydroponics system but it is a good way into the world of growing without soil) is just $89 on Amazon.com and hardly takes up any room – it is around the size of a medium-large houseplant.

Plants grown in the AeroGrow system will grow at 3 times the speed they would using traditional gardening methods.

The 'Farm In A Box Little Tokyo' system is $295 on Amazon. It can be used indoors or outdoors. It is neat – 28" x 18" x 18" – and weighs (empty) just 23 pounds.

Many people prefer to site their units outdoors as it reduces the need for artificial light, but then they need to think about protection for the fish over Winter, such as a greenhouse, garage, or polytunnel.

You could also design your own setup, to fit in with your specific needs. How about a small tank of fish with a piece of guttering housing the plants? Or making it a water feature and the focal point of your garden?

We are experimenting at home with making a garden system featuring a pond and a slate waterfall, surrounded by growbeds in a rockery style. This aquaponics stuff is seriously addictive!

The thing to remember is that you need much less space for an aquaponics system than you do for a traditional garden. A growbed can produce up to 20 times the produce that the same size of soil would produce in a traditional garden.

The plants will also grow more quickly than plants do in soil, so it is more cost-effective and space-effective than growing in soil.

MYTH 6 – IT'S COMPLICATED

It can seem a little complicated when you read about it. Get stuck in, though, and you start to enjoy it and realize what fun it is. Hands-on courses are available and are great for learning about aquaponics in a fun, practical way – and making friends with people with similar interests too.

All you need for the 'hardware' of a system are:

- Two tanks (one – the growbed - with a hole in if you want to site it above the fish tank);
- One frame [optional]. This is to stand the growing tank on top of the fish tank;
- One garden fountain-type pump;
- A fill pipe & filter and a siphon pipe (the return pipe);
- A hose to connect the pump to the fill pipe;
- A drain;

- The growing medium (e.g. clay pebbles or lava rock), planting pods (optional), testing kits (optional), fish, fish food, seeds or plants.

Traditional gardening is much more hard work than aquaponics – lots of digging for a start. I do a bit of soil gardening but to save the work of digging I have a large raised bed in my garden that I fill with compost each spring. I plant seeds in little paper pots and grow them on my kitchen windowsill. They need watering twice a day and checking that they aren't getting too much/too little sun.

Eventually they get big and strong enough to move outside to my little plastic greenhouse. Over the course of a couple of weeks, I start hardening them off by leaving the door open for longer, eventually all night. Then they're ready for the big outdoors – planting in the raised bed.

But that's not the end of it. I have to continually remove weeds (and often hens!) from the bed, check that they aren't too dry or waterlogged and water them as necessary – which is several times a day during hot spells.

None of that is needed when growing aquaponically. No digging, no watering, no fiddling around with seed pots, no transplanting, no hardening off.

If you use gravel in your growbed (the upper tank, the one without the fish), you can just sprinkle seeds over it.

Many people prefer a different growing medium, such as lava rock. Little planting pods can be used for the seeds/plants and popped between the lava rock.

You can still buy vegetable plants from garden centers to use in an aquaponics system. Plants bought for hydroponics systems are also perfect for aquaponics as you don't need to wash the compost from their roots.

THE SCIENCE STUFF

The fish produce waste;
The waste is turned by natural bacteria
in the water into nitrites and nitrates;
The nitrates feed the plants;
The plants filter and purify the water,
which goes back to the fish.

That's it!

The water that is pumped from the fish tank onto the plants in the growbed is full of nutrients that the plants need.

The plants act like a reed bed to remove harmful properties from the water, thereby purifying it for the fish.

The water is then oxygenated as it flows back into the fish tank. Which is why you have happy fish in an aquaponics system. The fish live in clean, healthy water and don't need all the medicines they seem to require when they live in aquariums.

Using the fish waste in this way is not only beneficial for the plants. Fish farms produce a lot of waste – sewage – which is bad for the environment because it is too much being released at once. They don't clean it up! Working with nature means there is no such thing as waste, it is all re-used. In an aquaponics system it is re-used by the plants, which yum it up.

The only vaguely sciencey bit is checking the water on a weekly basis. It isn't essential but it does help. It just involves using a simple kit and takes only minutes to do.

All you do is take a little water from the fish tank and put 3 drops from the kit into it, then match the color to a [supplied] chart.

If the pH is too high or low, you add things to bring it back down/up. pH Up & pH Down are inexpensive and they last a long time. If you don't overfeed your fish, and add a little extra water occasionally when evaporation pinches some, the pH levels should be quite stable.

I actually love testing the water, it makes me feel a bit like a scientist!

WHAT HAPPENS IN WINTER?

If you have an indoor system it will naturally be warmer, which will extend the growing season. There are also lots of plants which grow in winter (there must be, or we wouldn't have survived in ye olde days).

You can extend the season even more by buying special grow lights (like those commonly used in hydroponics) and/or heaters. You may find that you really like the lights. They need to be full-spectrum, and can make humans feel good, as well as fish! A lot of naturopathic doctors are recommending that we spend time using full-spectrum lights, not fluorescent ones.

Many people with outdoor aquaponics setups simply put them in a greenhouse or polytunnel, or add one over their setup in the Fall. This extends the growing season without needing to use heaters.

At home I use a temporary, plastic greenhouse which I erect over the aquaponics unit towards the end of summer when it is starting to get noticeably cool. It was very inexpensive in a local hardware store but it keeps the fish snug over winter. I don't add artificial heat, but that's because we prefer to eat seasonally. We don't want 'forced' plants, I want to eat plants in Winter that naturally grow in Winter. The aquaponics system and plastic greenhouse just keep them from being killed off by frost and snow.

We do find that plants thrive way beyond the normal growing season, even without artificial heat and light. We are in the North of England, which is known for its drizzle and lack of light. So if you are setting up an aquaponics system in sunny Sydney or Florida, you can probably expect year-round crops without too much intervention.

It surprised me – having been a fair-weather gardener before taking up aquaponics – just how many plants do grow during the cold months.

There are also lots of plants to sow during the colder months as well. We usually plant onions, garlic, peas, rocket and Winter lettuce, parsley, spinach, kale, and cabbage.

Planting in the late Fall means harvesting in January and February, which is lovely as the soil is often still frozen so it seems a luxury to be able to harvest plants.

We do protect the fish tank with bubble wrap (we buy it in a big roll, it isn't expensive), so they don't get too cold.

MYTH 7 – YOU CAN'T GROW MUCH

'The greatest fine art of the future will be the making of a comfortable living from a small piece of land.'
Abraham Lincoln

You would probably be surprised by just how much you can grow in an aquaponics system – both in terms of variety and quantity. Abraham Lincoln would be even more surprised!

There is a myth that only leafy green vegetables can be grown aquaponically. While they certainly can, they aren't the only things that can be grown.

WHAT YOU CAN GROW

There aren't many plants that can't be grown aquaponically. Here are some of the plants that people report the greatest success and volume with:

- Lettuce
- Cucumbers
- Tomatoes
- Onion*
- Watercress
- Celery
- Spinach
- Broccoli
- Pak choi
- Arugula
- Cabbage
- Garlic
- Most herbs
- Chilies
- Peas
- Beans
- Peppers
- Parsley and other leafy herbs such as basil
- Houseplants

Those are the plants that are most often grown aquaponically because they are so easy and quick, but other plants can be successfully grown as well, such as:

- Most berries
- Carrots (they tend to grow odd-shaped but taste wonderful)
- Beetroot
- Egg plant
- Squash
- Zucchini
- Millet

Plants that aren't generally grown in aquaponics systems tend to be the field crop plants such as wheat, potatoes, soybeans. People have reported success growing potatoes but you need a very deep growbed and they grow so well in soil that it is easier to plant them out in the garden if you have one.

Mint would grow well – it grows well anywhere … too well! It is a very invasive plant and would quickly take over your growbed if you let it. It could even extend its roots into the piping of the system, not great.

Don't forget flowers too. They grow prolifically aquaponically.

How Much Can You Grow?

It depends on the size of your system and how frequently you harvest and replant. You can produce very large quantities of produce.

You can plant seeds and seedlings much closer together than you would in soil. They aren't competing for nutrients, they extract all the nutrients they need from the water.

The seeds can be sprinkled onto the growbed or planted in grow pods. Seedlings and larger plants can also be planted in either the growbed or pods. A combination of sprinkled seeds and planted seedlings/plants works best as the larger seedlings/plants provide shelter for the germinating seeds. The seeds then grow slowly and really develop once the larger plants have been harvested. This is what happens in the rainforest.

In part of my raised bed I used to grow rows of beetroot, spinach, garlic and lettuce in the soil. I can plant 3 times the amount in my aquaponics system. Now, because they grow faster than in the soil, I can replant throughout the season and harvest even more.

DO THE PLANTS GET DISEASES LIKE GARDEN PLANTS?

In theory, they are subject to the same diseases but in practice they are much less likely to get them. It seems to be because they are well-fed, stronger, and away from soil-based bacteria.

*Onion. There is a problem at the moment in the UK with onion crops. A lethal disease – white rot - is wiping out onion plants. Respected consumer testing group Which? reported that once the disease has become established in soil it is impossible for gardeners to eliminate it.

Growing onion aquaponically is the ideal solution for those affected and for everyone who wants to avoid troubles with soil-based diseases for all their produce.

PART TWO

GETTING GOING

SETTING UP A SYSTEM

For a basic system you will need the following parts, which you can get from aquaponics suppliers, hydroponics suppliers, hardware stores, plumbing stores, garden suppliers, etc:

- 2 tanks – one for the plants (the growbed) and one for the fish.
- [Optional] A stand to place the growbed above the fish tank.
- A pump – to pump the water from the fish tank up to the growing tank. This sits in the fish tank.
- A siphon & drain – to allow the water to drain back down into the fish tank. This sits in the growing tank.
- A regulator – to determine the height the water gets to in the growing tank. This sits under the growing tank, on the fill pipe from the pump.
- Water tests – to get the right balance for the health of the fish,

- Growing medium – stones or pebbles. This is what the plants grow in. You can also get little pods for growing smaller seeds/plants in within the stones.
- Bacteria to add to the filter.
- Something to start the cycling process (you can use aged urine).
- Fish.
- Plants/seeds.
- And water, of course!

Optional extras:

- Plant pods (sometimes called Plugs). These are dinky little peat-like containers for growing seeds and small plants in.
- An air stone & pump (for the fish tank). This oxygenates the water even more – which is good because fish die quickly without enough oxygen. You can do without an air stone if you arrange your growbed so the water falls from a height and splashes into the fish tank.
- Decorative pond plants.
- Ornaments to provide shelter for fish.

- A cover for the fish tank (although this can be a bit more of a necessity than an optional extra, depending on where your system is sited.)
- A greenhouse or some type of surrounding structure if the system is outside.
- A light if the system is going to be kept indoors.

The system is quite self-regulating. It works a little like a reed bed – the plants purify the water for the fish, the fish provide nutrients for the plants (actually their waste is converted by bacteria in the water into nutrients for the plants).

Systems can vary a great deal depending on whether you are assembling a bought system or building your own DIY version but once you have some idea of how everything goes together you will be able to think about designing your own.

The main thing to remember is that they are not as complex as they first appear; a taskforce of a plumber and electrician will not be necessary!

Once you have set it up, you will need to leave it running, with just the water in the fish tank, for at least a week. This gives the bacteria chance to build up, ready to get to work on the fish waste once they arrive. You'll just need to keep an eye on it by doing a few water tests, so you'll know when it is ready for the fish.

CHECKLIST FOR SETTING UP A SYSTEM

B efore you start, you only need to choose the system itself and your growing medium. Fish and plants come later on.

TASK	NOTES
Set up the hardware – tanks, pipe work, pump, hose, etc.	
Choose, then clean the growing medium and add to the grow tank.	
Add water to the fish tank.	
Test the water using kits – pH, nitrites/nitrates, hardness.	
Add bacteria to the filter.	

Add something to encourage the natural cycling process, such as: aged urine, water from another aquaponic system, etc. Without this, you will need to wait a bit longer for the levels of bacteria to build up in the system.	
Leave for at least a week.	
Test the water and, once the levels are right, you can add fish.	
Choose and add 2-4 fish.	
Add plants/seeds.	
Feed the fish daily – but remember that the biggest cause of fish death is over-feeding. Follow the instructions carefully.	

Add more fish after 2 weeks.	
Harvest and enjoy the plants - within weeks.	
Keep planting throughout the growing season, a mixture of plants and seeds.	

Be sure to add the fish very gradually, just a few at a time, perhaps 2-4 fish every few weeks. This helps the system keep in balance and keeps the fish healthy.

If you have any questions about fish health, your supplier will be the best person to help as he/she will know your fish and your geographical area.

We tried a few local suppliers before we found someone we were happy with. He is passionate about fish, knowledgeable about their health, and enthusiastic about aquaponics. He's on speed dial!

Choosing The Growing Medium

The main factor to consider is the size of the stone or shale used. Stones of an average 10mm in size are best for a 4' tank, possibly going up to 20mm in a 6' or 8' tank.

RIVER STONE

This can be used as long as it doesn't contain large quantities of limestone, which would affect the hardness of the water. Brown river stone can be used but as per above, check that the size of the stone is suitable.

LAVA ROCK

This is good to use but can be hard to handle as it is abrasive. Make sure the lava rock doesn't come from the leftovers of any factory or industrial purpose as it could contain heavy metals which would kill your fish in no time. It will take extra washing.

PEA GRAVEL

Also known as pea shingle. This can be used but great care should be taken that it has not come from a building or industrial supplier. Many builders use pea gravel as a ballast in concrete so the quality needs to be checked thoroughly. Plants may not like to be planted directly in pea gravel which would mean you having to purchase "grow pods" for seeds or small plants (which you may prefer to do anyway).

GRANITE CHIPPINGS

Again, this would be a good stone to use but not only would it need a LOT of rinsing, it will be heavy, very heavy!

BLACK SHALE

This would **not** be suitable for an aquaponics system. The shale generates fine particles of dust which no amount of rinsing can remove. This would ruin your pump filter in no time as well as raising the pH so far that fish would not stand a chance.

SLATE CHIPPINGS

A possible alternative to river stone. Slate chippings need a lot of rinsing, would be heavy and has one main disadvantage; the edges of the chippings tend to be very sharp. Not only do plants struggle to get their roots through the stone, you also cut your fingers to ribbons! This is beside the fact that most places where slate chippings can be found in the wild are designated SSSI's, (Sites of Special Scientific Interest) and you could be breaking the law by collecting it.

A SUGGESTION

There are many dealers of stone/shingle/ballast/gravel who will be happy to supply sample bags of the stones that they supply. If you were to obtain a bag of each stone that you fancy trying, you could take it home, rinse it will distilled water and then check the pH level.

This would show whether the stone would then tend to be acidic or alkaline and can be treated accordingly.

In any case, after a few rinses, you would at least be able to see which is going to be the easiest to clean.

WHERE TO PUT THE SYSTEM

Whether you put your system indoors or outdoors depends on how much room you have and what you want to grow in it.

Some fish won't survive outside in Winter. It is best to get advice from fish breeders in your own local region.

LIGHT

Ideally, the system needs to have natural sunlight for much of the day. Without that, you need to think about providing artificial light. So if you are setting your system up outside in the garden, pick a spot, if you can, that gets good light for much of the day.

The light is for the plants, not the fish. The fish don't need sunlight – it encourages algae – so some sort of lid on the fish tank is a good idea if the tank is going to be kept outdoors.

You can also buy pond plants that float. These are a good natural way of limiting the amount of sunlight that reaches the fish. It also makes life more fun for them, they like swimming through them and hiding under them. Fish in tanks with plants tend to be healthier, as they are in cleaner water and are less stressed.

If you are putting your system in a garage, you will need to look into getting some lights and setting them up above the growing tank. Check out aquarium suppliers and pet stores. There are good bulbs that provide the next best thing to natural daylight.

Artificial light shouldn't be necessary if your system is going to be housed in a greenhouse but if you do add a few bulbs, you can extend the growing season.

Many people report that full spectrum bulbs cause plants to grow at an incredible rate.

Be careful not to site the system under trees or large plants. They can contaminate the water. There are lots of plants that are toxic to fish. It's best to be cautious and only allow pond plants in or near your system.

ACCESS TO ELECTRICITY

The system does need to be plugged in, to run the pump. It is possible to use an extension cable for this – just be sure to get one that is suitable for outdoor, all-weather use.

If you are setting the system up indoors, this isn't a problem, of course. You just need to site it near enough to a socket so that you aren't tripping over the cable.

If the area you live in suffers from regular power cuts, you may want to consider a backup system to keep the pump running, otherwise the fish could suffer.

Fish For Aquaponics

Many types of fish will live happily in an aquaponics system. The type you choose will come down to where in the world you live, where you situate your system, whether you are going to heat the water and whether you are going to eat the fish or keep them as pets.

It is best to choose a breed of fish that is native to where you live – they will be used to the climate.

Check with your fish supplier whether they are suitable for cold water, if not you will need to find a method of heating the water and keeping the tank warm from outside air.

Only add a maximum of 4 fish at a time, then another 4 in a couple of weeks time. You can stock a maximum (in weight) of 1lb of fish in 5-10 gallons of water. Some experts suggest an inch of fish per gallon of water, or two and a half gallons of water per average fish.

Here is a run-through of some of the most popular types of fish that people have had success with in aquaponics systems (sorted alphabetically):

- Brown Trout
- Carp
- Catfish
- Goldfish
- Guppies
- Koi
- Large Mouth Bass
- Mollies
- Pacu
- Perch
- Sunfish
- Swordfish
- Tench
- Tetras
- Tilapia

Tilapia are one of the most popular fish to grow aquaponically, as they are hardy (they don't mind a bit of overcrowding) and edible. They do, however, prefer warmer water, so aren't suitable for outdoor systems in northern/cold areas.

Trout are quite popular because they are a delicacy, although they aren't as easy to raise.

Goldfish are inexpensive and popular with people who don't want to eat their fish.

Some people also like to add a few clams to their fish tank – apparently they keep the tank clean.

PLANTS THAT ARE TOXIC TO FISH

I t's lovely to have an aquaponic system photogenically set up beneath a tree. But that tree could poison your fish. The list of plants that are toxic to fish is LONG. To be safe, it is best to keep your system completely away from garden plants.

I made the mistake of putting mine next to a privet hedge and some lilies. Bad move. Both are lethal for fish. I keep the lid permanently on my fish tank now. It has vents to allow light and air in but not so much light that will allow algae to build up.

Here are some links to sites that list the plants that are toxic to fish. It is best to check in your own country to see if there are any local plants not listed by these sites.

- http://en.wikipedia.org/wiki/Fish_toxins

- http://www.splashtastic-aquatics.net/poisonous-plants-pond-garden

- http://forum.practicalfishkeeping.co.uk/archive/index.php/t-14222.html

- http://www.homeservicesengine.com/articles/tips_guide_to_poisonous_plants.html

DIY PLANS

There are both free and paid DIY plans for making your own aquaponics system available online.

One of the most innovative is the Barrel-Ponics system, which uses 3 barrels and some plumbing materials. The plans are free, from Faith & Sustainable Technologies:

http://bit.ly/barrelponics

The UK-based site AquaponicWorld also supply instructions for setting up a DIY system:

http://aquaponicworld.com/diy/

There is a good plan on this site using bits and pieces from IKEA and a plumbing store:

http://www.wikihow.com/Make-a-DIY-Indoor-Aquaponics-System

FAQ

DO I NEED A GREENHOUSE?

It isn't essential unless you live in a very cold area - if you do you will need some sort of protection for your fish in the freezing winter months.

I use an inexpensive plastic greenhouse that is like a small polytunnel. There are problems with plastic greenhouses – they tend to blow away in windy weather – but you can get round a lot of them by careful siting and tying down. The covers perish after a few years but they aren't expensive to replace.

The main benefit of a greenhouse is that you can grow more delicate crops, and extend the growing season. A greenhouse means that your system can be in full production year-round. It provides protection for both fish and plants from cold.

You would need to consider putting some lights in during the darker months, though, if you want to grow right through the winter.

I managed to get hold of some bubble wrap, which we wrap around the fish tank in Winter, just to give them a bit of extra protection.

IS AQUAPONICS COST-EFFECTIVE?

Aquaponics is more cost-effective than growing in soil, for numerous reasons:

- Less water use. A study by the Australian government found aquaponics to be the world's most productive food system in terms of water use efficiency (http://www.pc.gov.au/__data/assets/pdf_file/0005/15359/sub046.pdf).
- Less chemical use (apart from the kits to test the water).
- Less pesticide use.
- Less running costs, if compared to conventional farming.
- Can produce both fish and plants all year round, using a greenhouse.

There are increased running costs with using a system indoors, for the lighting, but this is fairly minimal.

WHY IS THE PH SO IMPORTANT?

pH stands for 'parts Hydrogen' (actually opinions vary on what the 'p' stands for, with some saying 'power of' but 'parts' is easier to understand).

Hydrogen is represented by a capital H in science.

Water is H_2O – which is made up of two parts hydrogen to every part of oxygen. Water is pH neutral (pH 7). Something with a pH of less than 7 is said to be acidic; more than 7 it is said to be basic or alkaline.

The less parts Hydrogen something has, the more acidic it is. H_2O_2 – hydrogen peroxide – can be a strong acid. It is a bleach. That is made up of one part of Hydrogen to every one part of oxygen. The pH varies depend on the strength of the H_2O_2 solution.

So if you had something like bleach in the water with your fish, it is understandable that that would not be good for their health.

But in the same say you don't want too many parts Hydrogen either. It is just as dangerous, in different ways. Something of pH 14 is just as dangerous as pH 1, just in a different way.

Keeping the pH at the right level for your fish is therefore very important.

(Thanks to my scientifically-minded daughter, Anna Maria, for explaining this at a level I could understand!)

HOW OFTEN SHOULD I TEST THE WATER?

Ideally, test the pH weekly. You will be able to tell if the balance is off by the health of both the fish and the plants, but you can find out before they get ill by testing the water. The pH needs to be around 7.0-7.6 for the nitrification process to take place. If it drops below 7.0, the bacteria stop reproducing and the ammonia levels rise.

If it is too high (too alkaline), it helps to plant more seeds/plants. If it is too low (too acid), it can help to remove any very large plants – or those with large root systems.

There are products available for altering the pH of the water. Be careful to add them gradually. I have found the best method is to add the product to a bucket of water and add some of the contents of the bucket to the grow tank (i.e. not directly on the fish) over the course of a day or so. Otherwise you can shock the system and cause other things to go out of balance.

You can do the other tests – ammonia, nitrites, nitrates - less frequently. Perhaps monthly. If the ammonia levels are too high, take out some of the water (up to 1/3) and replace it with fresh water.

If the water looks cloudy, try not feeding the fish for a day or two (they will survive that).

The testing kits aren't expensive and they last for quite a while.

DO YOU HAVE TO USE FRESH WATER? CAN I USE SALTWATER?

Some people do use saltwater – obviously with saltwater fish – but you would be limited in what you could grow in a saltwater system. Seaweeds mainly!

Aquaponics Shop (http://www.aquaponics-shop.com) report success with a saltwater system. They use barramundi fish and grow ulva (sea lettuce).

Saltwater fish can get ill if kept in captivity, so I think this is one for experienced fish keepers only.

WHERE CAN I BUY FISH FOR MY SYSTEM?

Pet stores and aquarium supply stores carry fish. The staff are usually knowledgeable about which fish will live happily together.

Be sure to tell them that you are buying them to put in an aquaponics system.

You can also buy fish online. Search for fish hatcheries and suppliers in your area.

WHAT DO THE FISH EAT?

Basic fish food, available from pet/aquatic stores and animal food suppliers. Take advice from your supplier as certain fish prefer certain types of food – flakes, sticks, insects, algae, worms, etc.

The main thing with the food is not to overdo it. Stick to the instructions carefully. They will probably need less food in cold weather. If you overfeed them they can not only get ill, but there will be waste food, which can go off and affect the water quality.

WHY CAN'T I ADD ALL THE FISH AT ONCE?

Only adding a few fish at a time allows the bacteria in the system to build up gradually. They grow quite slowly. If you add all the fish in one go, it will overwhelm the system – the bacteria won't be numerous enough to cope with all the fish waste. The end result would be fish illness and possibly death.

WHAT SHOULD I DO IF MY FISH LOOK ILL?

Firstly, test the water. Then make sure that no garden plants are dropping leaves or needles in the system. Recheck the instructions on the fish food, to make sure you aren't feeding them too much (they will need less food in cold weather). Check that the air pump in the fish tank is aerating the water – it is how they get oxygen. Add air stones if necessary because the fish will die without enough oxygen.

The company that supplied your fish may be willing to test the water for you – often free of charge. They often have more advanced testing facilities, and a wider range of things they can check.

An Internet search in your country can bring up useful fish health sites.

Here's one:

http://www.fishdoc.co.uk/disease/
diseasehome.htm

Fish are cold blooded and can't regulate their own body temperature. So if the water isn't at the right temperature for them, they can get ill/diseased.

Protect them from the shock of sudden noise, movement, and light. Allowing children to run around, banging into the fish tank, is a sure way to stress your fish, which can make them ill.

Fish have a natural lifespan, so you will lose some occasionally, but if they all get sick at once it is sign of something wrong.

It is upsetting to lose fish, but you can usually learn from it and make sure it doesn't happen again. It can be that you have bought a bad batch of fish – already infected with something – that have affected your others.

WHAT POND PLANTS ARE SUITABLE FOR AQUAPONIC SYSTEMS?

Plants aren't essential but if you have a problem with sunlight entering your fish tank, then floating plants can be helpful. Some plants are good for the fish too, they enjoy nibbling them. Any pond/aquatic plants that you can buy locally should be fine. You can even find aquatic plants on EBay.

Some of the most popular are:

- Duckweed – very fast-growing and enjoyed by fish. Some people complain that bits break off and end up in the growbed but I haven't had this problem, I think I have greedy fish!

- Hornwort
- Najas grass
- Wolffia

Check any plants you buy very carefully for snails before putting them in your tank.

I HAVE A LARGE POND. CAN I USE IT AS PART OF AN AQUAPONICS SYSTEM?

It is possible – as long as they pond isn't fed from a stream - but you are likely to encounter quite a few problems. (A pond fed from a stream means flowing water, and the fish waste would get diluted and washed away, so the plants wouldn't thrive.)

The bacteria that make the aquaponics system work are light-sensitive and may be less effective or even killed by the light that naturally enters a pond. You could solve this by shading your pond.

You would need to aerate the water to get good dissolved oxygen levels.

If the pond is very big and you wanted to harvest the fish from it, you would need extra equipment - nets, wetsuits, etc.

HOW SHOULD I REMOVE THE CHLORINE FROM THE WATER BEFORE I ADD THE FISH?

The best way is to wait for a week after filling the tank before adding the fish. Chlorine is a gas and will disappear into the air.

I HEARD OF PEOPLE USING WORMS IN THEIR TANKS. IS THAT OK?

Some commercial growers use them, they are good for dealing with any fish waste that gets through to the growbed unaltered by the bacteria. They aren't really necessary for non-commercial systems.

WILL CLEANING THE TANKS BE TEDIOUS?

No. Cleaning them in the way that you would an indoor aquarium – completely changing the water and disinfecting the tank - would remove the vital bacteria that are needed to convert the fish waste into plant nutrients.

All you need to do is manually remove any floating debris and use a brush to scrub the walls and bottom occasionally. The water will go a bit murky but the pump should deal with it and it will clear again within a few days.

CAN I USE POTTED PLANTS THAT HAVE BEEN RAISED IN SOIL?

Yes, I do this all the time. You need to be careful to wash off as much of the soil/compost as possible. Young plants with loose soil are easily rinsed clean but clay-type soil or older plants takes a bit more time. It does come off though. A soak (in fresh water) helps.

Also, inspect the plants for insects or aphids before adding them to your system. If in doubt, grow your own plants from seed. This can be done in the aquaponic growbed, by putting the seeds into grow plugs (available from aquaponic and hydroponic suppliers). You can actually sprinkle seeds straight onto your growing medium. I've done this with success too, but it is a bit more hit and miss, because they get moved around during each flooding, as the system floods and drains. You never know where they are going to end up!

WHAT IF I SEE BUGS ON MY PLANTS?

It is important to look out for harmful bugs. Second, see if you can identify what bugs you are dealing with. Large ones can be dealt with manually by picking them off the plants.

The best thing to do - If your plants are small enough – is to remove them from the growing medium and soak them in the fish tank for about 15 minutes. This drowns the bugs and gives the fish a treat, as they quite like bugs.

CAN I USE PESTICIDES ON THE PLANTS IN MY AQUAPONIC SYSTEM?

No, as they can kill the fish, even organic pesticide.

You can deal with most problems by keeping the water at the optimal levels for ammonia, pH, nitrites and nitrates. If plants have damaged leaves – e.g. mildew on tomato leaves – then remove the leaves. Some people report success with spraying a solution of milk on the leaves of plants that are susceptible to fungus.

AM I LIKELY TO GET COMPLAINTS FROM NEIGHBORS?

They won't have cause to complain – there is no more noise than from a normal pond pump. Toss them the odd lettuce if they are prone to grumpiness.

DOES AN AQUAPONICS SYSTEM CREATE NASTY SMELLS?

No, there is no smell because the fish waste is dealt with by the bacteria in the water and used by the plants. All the systems I have seen have smelt fresh and invigorating, actually. It's the abundance of green leaves I think.

CAN I PLANT IN MY SYSTEM RIGHT AWAY?

Not until you have got the system cycling. That can take anything from a week to a month. You'll know by testing the water.

You can plant as soon as you introduce some fish – in fact you should do so in order to start providing filtration for the fish.

Surprisingly, urine is one of the best ways of getting your system going! People have reported that it can take 4 days to get an ammonia reading if you use fresh urine, but much quicker – within a day – if you use aged urine. Try to find someone who doesn't take any medication (good luck with that!) and store their urine in a bucket for a few days before adding it to your system over the course of a few days. You don't need a lot. It will get it off to a flying start. Don't worry about smell, it is too dilute to be a problem.

CAN I GROW WITHOUT FISH?

No. I lost my fish in the early days (due to nearby privets and lilies dropping leaves into the tank – I felt so bad that my lack of knowledge killed my fish).

The plants in the growbed were thriving so I left them growing. I didn't get new fish as I hadn't yet determined what had killed the old ones. The plants soon withered and died. It was very interesting to see just how important the fish are to an aquaponics system.

You can grow plants hydroponically – you need to add fertilizer or liquid feed to the water to supply the bacteria in the water with ammonia. That's a whole other subject though!

WHY DON'T THE ROOTS OF THE PLANTS ROT? THEY ARE IN WATER NEARLY ALL THE TIME!

The roots of your plants probably look like they are permanently in water but actually they aren't, the flood and drain system means that they get a big soaking of water, then it drains away. Don't forget that they are growing in rocks substances (rocks, stones, clay pebbles). If they didn't have the regular rush of water they would dry out very quickly. The water that floods them is full of nutrients that they use.

Plants in soil have to sit in soil all the time to enable them to get the nutrients out of it. They may dry out, they may get waterlogged, they may pick up soil-borne diseases. Plants in an aquaponics system get flooded with nutrient-rich water regularly and then drained. They never dry out, they never get waterlogged ad they don't get soil-borne diseases. So they have pretty much ideal living conditions.

HOW MANY PLANTS SHOULD I GROW?

I haven't been able to find any research that gives exact ratios but it depends on the number and size of the fish. Two small goldfish aren't going to produce enough waste to support 50 big plants. Plant slowly and build up gradually.

It doesn't matter too much though. Too many plants won't kill the fish, the plants just won't be very healthy as they won't be getting enough nutrients. You will be able to tell very easily just by looking at them.

I have had a full growbed flourishing with a tank of just 6 goldfish (not massive fish, but not tiddly ones either). The plants included herbs, lettuce, broccoli, maize (surprisingly successful, that), and peas (I love peas and grow lots). So I don't think you need to hold back too much on the planting as long as you have more than about 4 fish.

DO PLANTS GROW FASTER IN AQUAPONIC SYSTEMS?

They sure do. You can almost see them growing!

Plants grow faster hydroponically than they do in soil and they grow even faster aquaponically. An aquaponic system will tend to produce plants that grow about twice as fast as they would in soil. Some plants grow even faster.

It seems to be because they get lots of water, all the time, as well as constant nutrients. They also don't have to deal with the usual pests in the soil either. They are growing in almost perfect conditions, so they tend to grow big, fast and strong.

Resources

Here are some resources – websites, books, and courses – for aquaponics in particular and self-sufficiency in general.

WEBSITES

BACKYARD AQUAPONICS	http://www.backyard aquaponics.com/
FRIENDLY AQUAPONICS	http://www.friendly aquaponics.com/ You can purchase plans for DIY aquaponics systems and solar greenhouses.
APPROPEDIA	http://www.appropedia.org /Aquaponics
WINDWARD	http://www.windward.org/ 2.0/index.php Sustainable living research and education center
SELF-SUFFICIENTISH	http://www.self sufficientish.com

RECOMMENDED BOOKS & COURSES

BOOKS

- How To Build And Take Care Of An Aquaponic Garden – AJ Clarke
- Urban Farming: Sustainable City Living In Your Backyard – Thomas J Fox
- Building An Aquaponics System – Anthony D Faircloth
- Rain Barrels, Chicken Coops And Solar Panels – Instructables Authors
- The Good Food Revolution – Will Allen & Charles Wilson
- How To Build Your Own Greenhouse – Roger Marshall
- Self Sufficiency For The 21st Century – Dick Strawbridge
- DIY Projects For The Self-Sufficient Homeowner: 25 Ways To Build A Self-Reliant Lifestyle – Betsy Matheson
- Maximizing Your Mini Farm – Brett L Markham

ONLINE COURSE

- Aquaponic Garden: Growing Fish & Vegetables Together – Sylvia Bernstein (http://ude.my/c47ef).

AQUAPONICS ORGANIZATIONS

US

Aquaponics Association
http://aquaponicsassociation.org/

Alternative Farming Systems Information Centre
http://afsic.nal.usda.gov/aquaculture-and-soilless-farming/aquaponics

Green Acre Aquaponics
http://greenacreaquaponics.com/

The Aquaponic Source
http://theaquaponicsource.com/2011/09/01/aquaponics-association/.
Information/resources

EUROPE

Aquaponic World
   http://www.aquaponicworld.com

Aquaponics UK
   http://www.aquaponics.org.uk

AUSTRALIA/NEW ZEALAND

Aquaponics Australia
   http://www.aquaonics.com.au/

JAPAN

Japan Aquaponics
   http://www.japan-aquaponics.com/

REST OF THE WORLD

Africa Aquaponics
   http://africaaquaponics.com/

WHAT'S NEXT?

What are you reasons for thinking about taking up aquaponics?

Some reasons people are:

- Financial – food costs have risen sharply. Growing some of your own food is financially astute. The savings really add up.

- Health – many people are becoming concerned about the quality of the food they buy. The spread of genetically-modified plants means they are part of our diets without us even realizing. If that is an issue for you, aquaponics could be a solution. Growing your own plants in an aquaponics system means they are about as healthy as they can get – totally organic and bursting with nutrients.

- Taste – many people complain that food doesn't taste as good as it used to. Watery strawberries, tasteless tomatoes, bland cucumbers. Growing your own makes a massive difference to the taste.

- Environmental – large-scale commercial production of food uses massive amounts of energy and is unsustainable.

- Work – growing food in the ground takes a lot of work, digging, hoeing, weeding, etc. None of those are needed with aquaponics. Those with limited mobility and/or limited time find that an aquaponics system is very liberating and allows them to grow foods that they wouldn't have considered using traditional gardening/growing methods.

- Social – there are small and large-scale aquaponics ventures run by community groups and others to help provide good, fresh food at affordable prices.

- Family – growing plants together and teaching children where food comes from is very rewarding. They quickly learn the basics of aquaponics, enjoy feeding and watching the fish, and are much more likely to eat the plants that they have grown themselves. It's a fun and sneaky way of getting children to eat vegetables!

- Future-proofing – remember all the worry about the Millennium bug, when the world's computer systems were expected to break down at the stroke of midnight as the 20th century turned into the 21st? It didn't happen but the concern was that food delivery systems would have been affected and large-scale food shortages would have hit the stores within a few days. It doesn't take a Millennium bug to cause problems like that. Climate change has caused many areas to have regular difficulties with drought or floods which cut off whole towns and villages from food supplies. Being able to grow some of your own food is comforting, knowing that food supplies can be shut off without warning. Having some degree of self-sufficiency brings with it the knowledge that you can provide for yourself and your family if disaster should come a little too close to home.

Whatever your reason, aquaponics could be a great hobby for you. Growing aquaponically is economical, healthy, and fun. It could even be profitable. You could sell at farmer's markets, direct to the public, even to local stores. Some people use their produce to barter for other goods or services.

Enjoy your aquaponic journey, wherever it takes you.

POSTSCRIPT – MY STORY

People discover aquaponics in different ways and for different reasons. Here is my story!

I had a bad car wreck in my early 20s that left me facially scarred, partially disabled, and needing multiple operations to rebuild my face and damaged intestines. There's nothing like chronic pain for awakening an interest in health!

I wanted to improve my diet and find natural ways of controlling pain – I hated being in the brain-numbing fog that comes with long-term painkiller use.

I was eventually diagnosed with Chronic Fatigue Syndrome in 1998. I hated the label, it made me feel like a malingerer. I battled it for over a decade, throwing everything I could at it, but nothing made much difference. Meeting others with the illness helped. They were, without exception, intelligent, former achievers. Several had been amateur athletes. All struggled with the diagnosis.

The best advice I got from the hospital was to do with adrenaline. Like all CFS sufferers, I had bleak days where I could hardly move, then I would have a slight lifting of the weariness and, knowing that it might not last long, would rush around trying to cram as much as possible in. That's totally the wrong thing to do. It is running on adrenaline. One of the questions they asked was if getting into an argument gave you a burst of energy. Everybody said yes. That's an adrenaline rush.

It's fine in an emergency, but do it day after day and you start to feel dreadful.

Adrenaline is a hormone that is released when your body senses danger or you have been through a traumatic experience. Adrenaline causes your body to release sugar into your bloodstream, giving a burst of energy. It is what you need to run away from trouble, to keep going when you're too tired to continue (e.g. for parents with wakeful babies and it is very useful.

It also gives you strength. When he was a teenager, my ex husband saw a wall fall onto a little girl. He lifted it up – many of the bricks held together – and rescued her. Afterwards he went back to the scene to show his parents and tried to life the wall again. He couldn't. The rush had worn off once the immediate danger was over.

The trouble is, if you live on adrenaline, if you rely on that as your only source of energy, your body struggles to deal with it afterwards. When the burst of energy has run out, you feel worse than ever. For me the worst thing was horrendous pain in the front of my thighs.

For people with health problems, once the adrenaline rush is over, the pain hits. You find yourself unable to sleep, your brain buzzes and won't let things go, you mull over every imagined slight. The lack of sleep puts you into zombie mode, where life is barely lived.

In a desperate attempt to find some energy, many people with adrenaline problems crave sugar and other refined carbohydrates. This of course means inevitable weight gain.

Eventually I found the Lightning Process, a training programme to help people cope with stress and recover from chronic illness. What was even better was the therapist I found. Jane (http://www.renaissance-training.com/janestory) had used LP to recover from CFS herself, and she had lost a large amount of weight too, using the LP thought processes.

Part of the process of recovering was to close my business – it was ruining my health – take up writing again and take up new hobbies.

Money was very tight and I was eating a lot of green vegetables so I decided to learn how to grow them. I had very little success with growing in soil - our soil is very clay-based and gets water-logged. I would forget to harvest things at the right time and find them rotting days later.

Since discovering aquaponics, I have been able to save money by growing a lot of my own veg and some fruit (although I don't eat as much fruit as I used to – I was craving the sugar before). My system is right outside my back door so I can easily see when things are ready to be harvested – I never leave things to rot in the growbed.

It's just so easy to harvest them, they are at waist height too so there isn't any bending or messy soil.

My diet is more alkaline now with all the green veg and I feel more calm and balanced. I'm happy and healthier for having such an abundance of organic produce in my diet - it is far cheaper to grow it than buy it.

So aquaponics has had a major effect on my lifestyle. I hope it helps you too.

My Health Habits

The things that have worked for me and that I continue to do:

- **Vegetarian**, low acid eating. I use pulses for a lot of cooking (lentil soup, quinoa & veg side dishes, nut & bean loaves).
- Regular **swimming**.
- Daily time **outdoors**. I live in the UK, where much of the population is chronically deficient in Vitamin D. Although we get sun in Winter, lovely days sometimes, it isn't bright enough to make sufficient Vitamin D. So I use a daylight lamp and take Vitamin D supplements from October-March.
- Gentle (all I can manage!) **rebounding**.
- **Skin brushing** (the subject of my book, 'The 10-Day Skin Brushing Detox'), this has had a massive effect on my health and my skin.
- **Oil pulling**.

- Eliminating **caffeine**.
- Reducing **sugar**. It is way too inflammatory. When I'm sugar-free, my joint pain is almost eliminated.
- Deep, relaxed **breathing**.
- **Positive mental outlook**. Letting go of hurts (real and imagined) and forgiving (self and others) made a huge difference.
- **Prayer**.
- Regular **massages**.
- Time away from **electrical gadgets**. I'm a computer geek. I do recognize, though, that technology isn't good for health. I need to put it down occasionally and go and look at the big sky. Being outdoors is the best thing for my health.
- **Dogs**! My dogs keep me smiling, keep me going outside when I don't feel like it and give me lots of love and cuddles. They are also great socializers – when you walk a dog you meet all the dog lovers in your town!

ABOUT THE AUTHOR

Michelle Booth was born to a book-mad mother and a bemused father. One of her earliest memories is of her Mom sitting on the floor reading, with a vacuum cleaner next to her. She had spotted an interesting book while cleaning, picked it up and got engrossed! Michelle feels the same – the vacuuming can wait.

She also remembers her Dad stepping over a pile of books, saying, "If you love them so much, why don't you try writing one?"

She did ... and hasn't stopped since. She is a former teacher who now writes books and courses for herself and other people.

BOOKS

- The 10-Day Skin Brushing Detox.
- Mo – The Talking Dog. A novel for children aged around 8-12 years old.
- Goodreads for Authors.

UDEMY.COM COURSES

- Goodreads for Authors.
- How to get your book on CreateSpace.

FREE EBOOKS

Amazon allow authors to have 5 days of offering their eBooks free, so they can let book reviewers and review sites know.

If you would like to receive notification when Michelle releases new books, please email her. She will let you know when the free days are scheduled.

To be added to the Free Book Alert list, please send an email to: michelleboothauthor@gmail.com with FREE BOOK LIST in the subject line.

If you can spare a few minutes, she would be very grateful for a quick review on Amazon.

INDEX

31089307R00074

Made in the USA
Lexington, KY
30 March 2014